A Mothers Love

De-stress coloring book

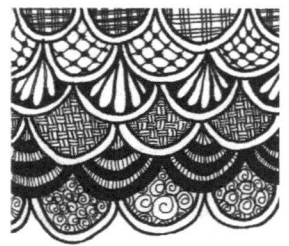

By Deleena Foster

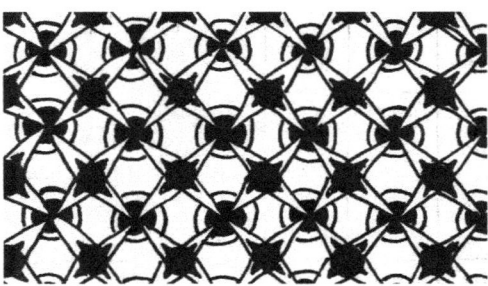

A Mothers Love: 20 Greyscale Hand Drawn Images, Adult Color Book
Copyright 2015 Deleena Foster
www.facebook.com/lovetanglearts
Check out other beautiful products for sale.

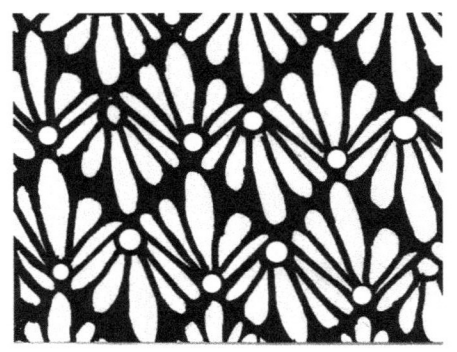

To
Wyatt & Odyn

MY LOVES, MY LIFE,
MY INSPIRATION,
MY EVERYTHING.
I'LL LOVE YOU FOREVER.

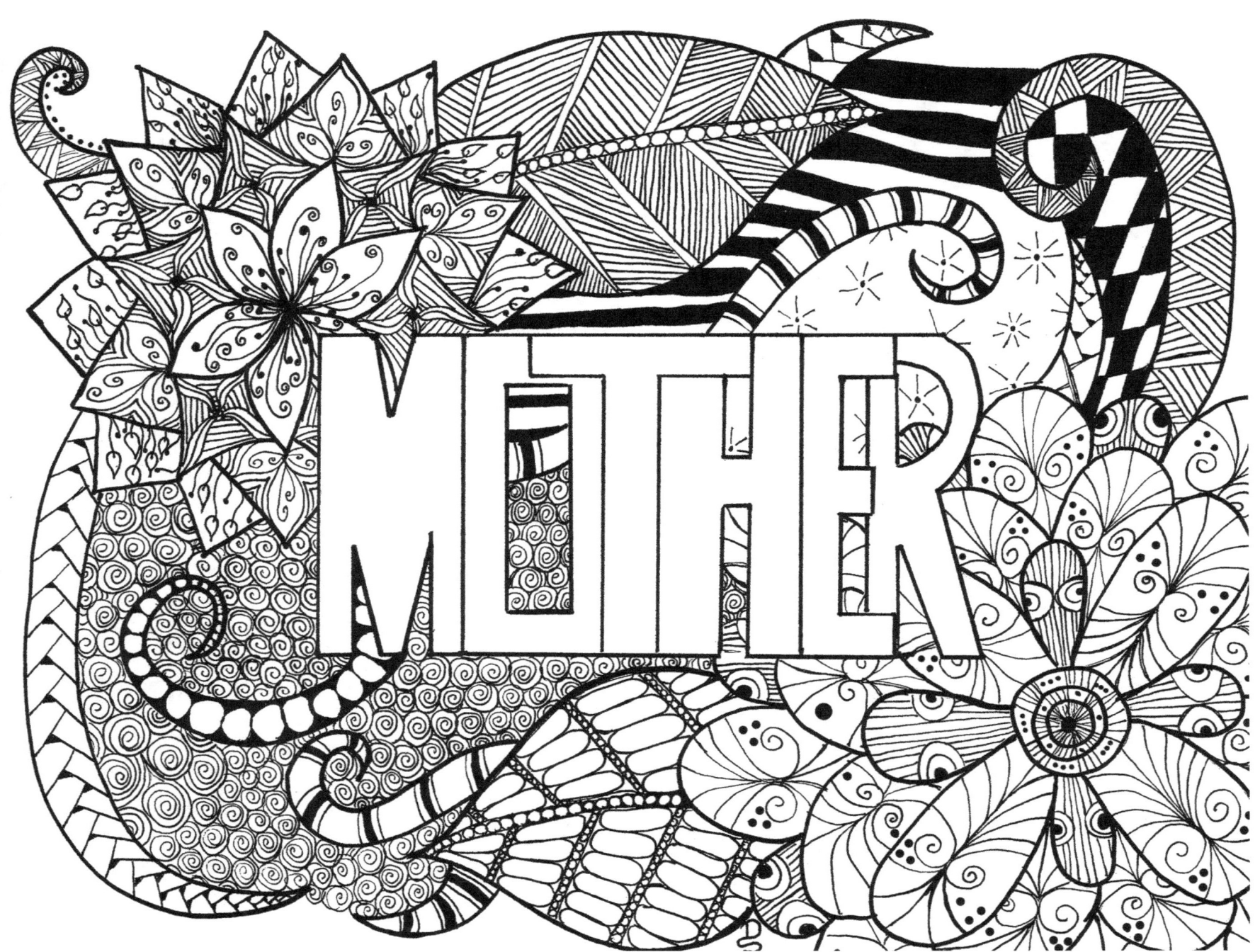

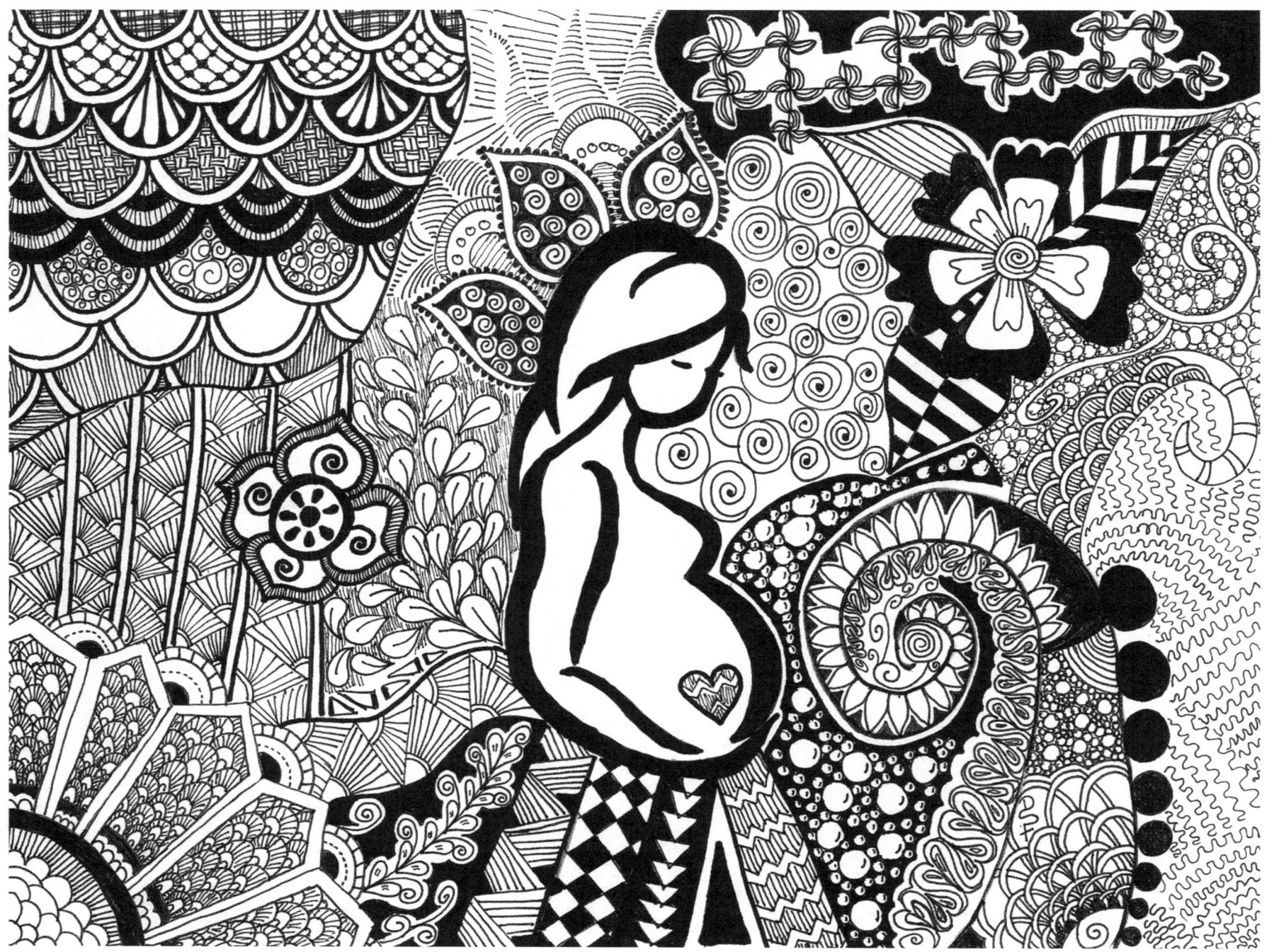

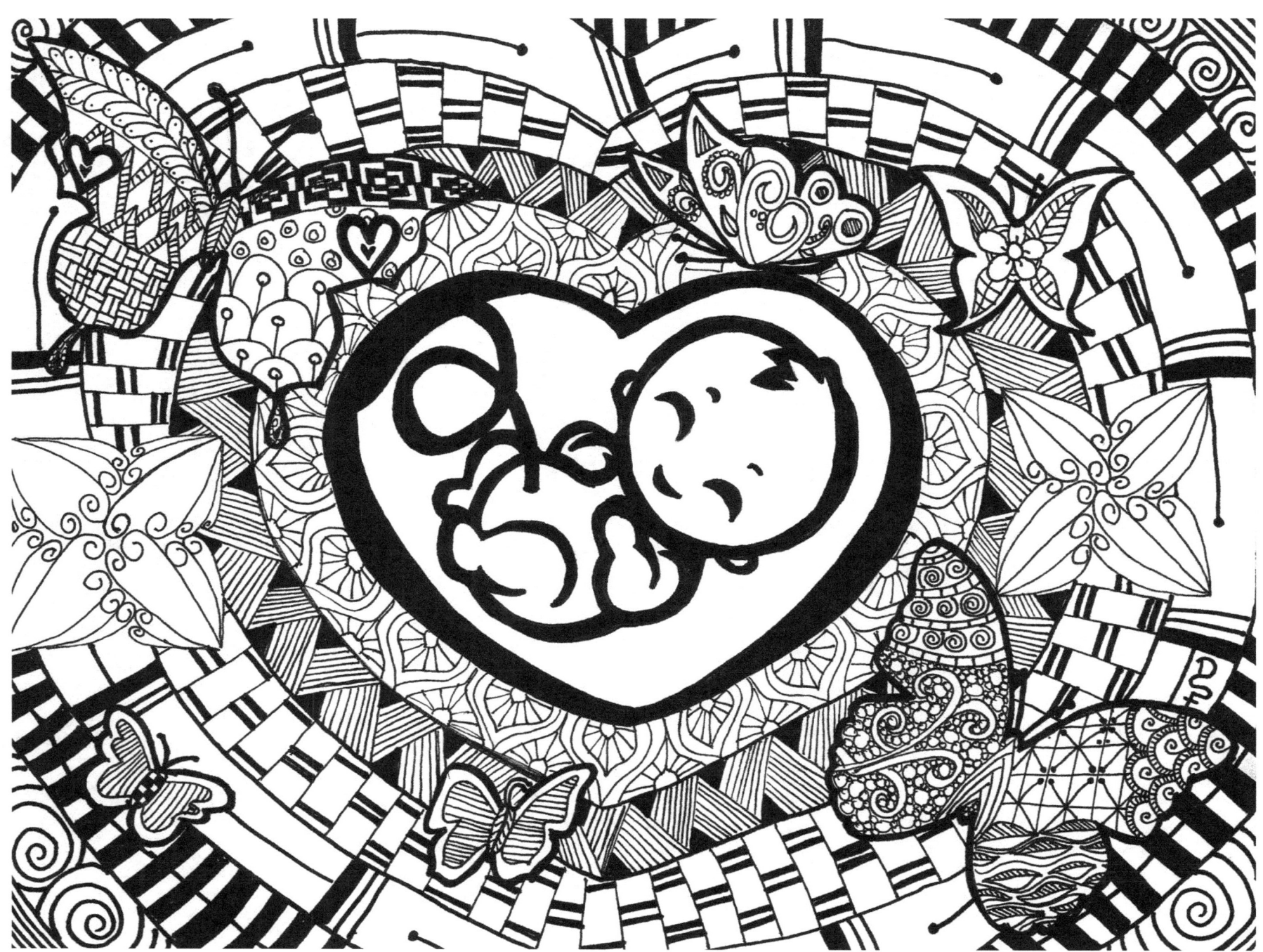

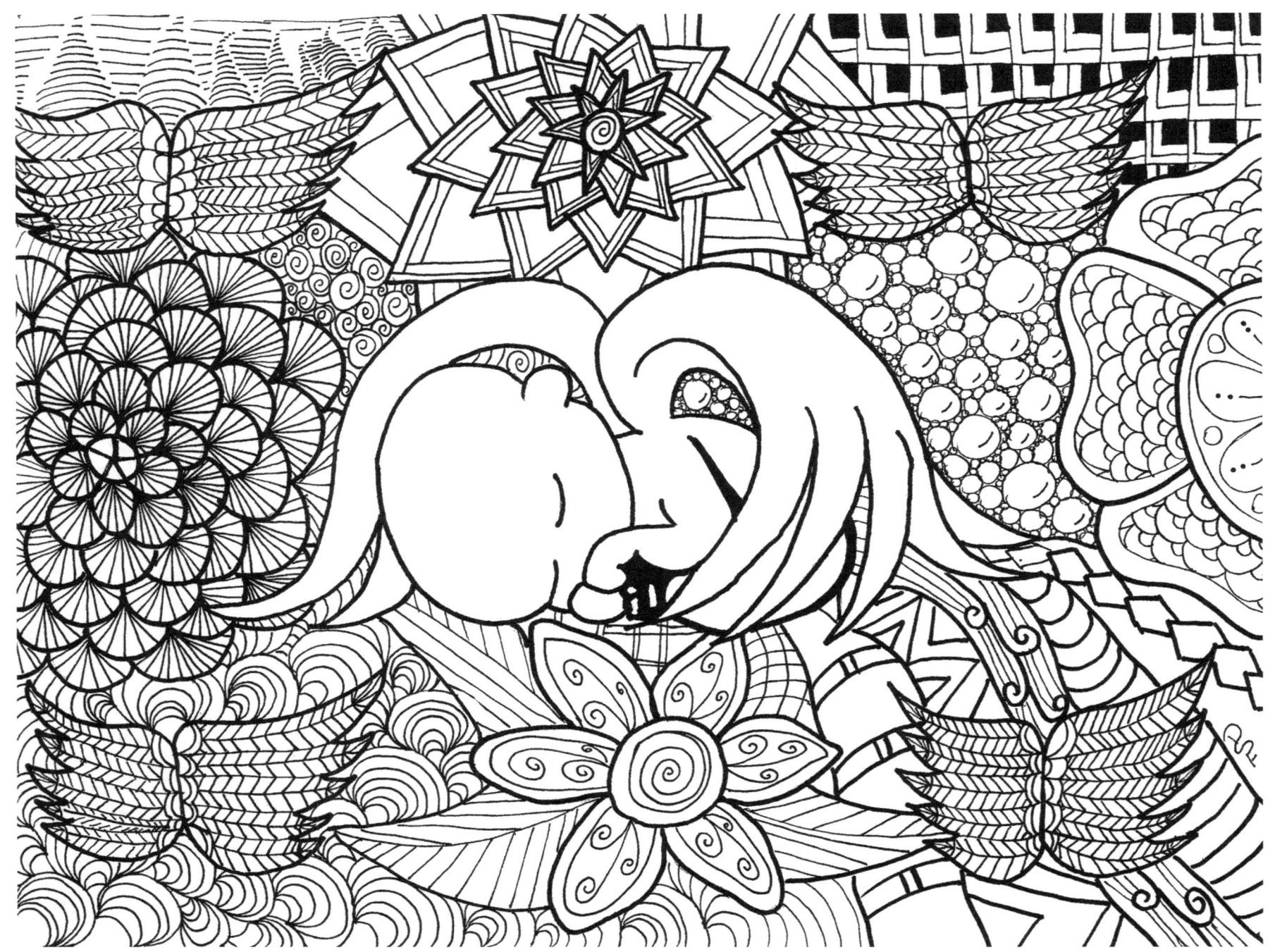

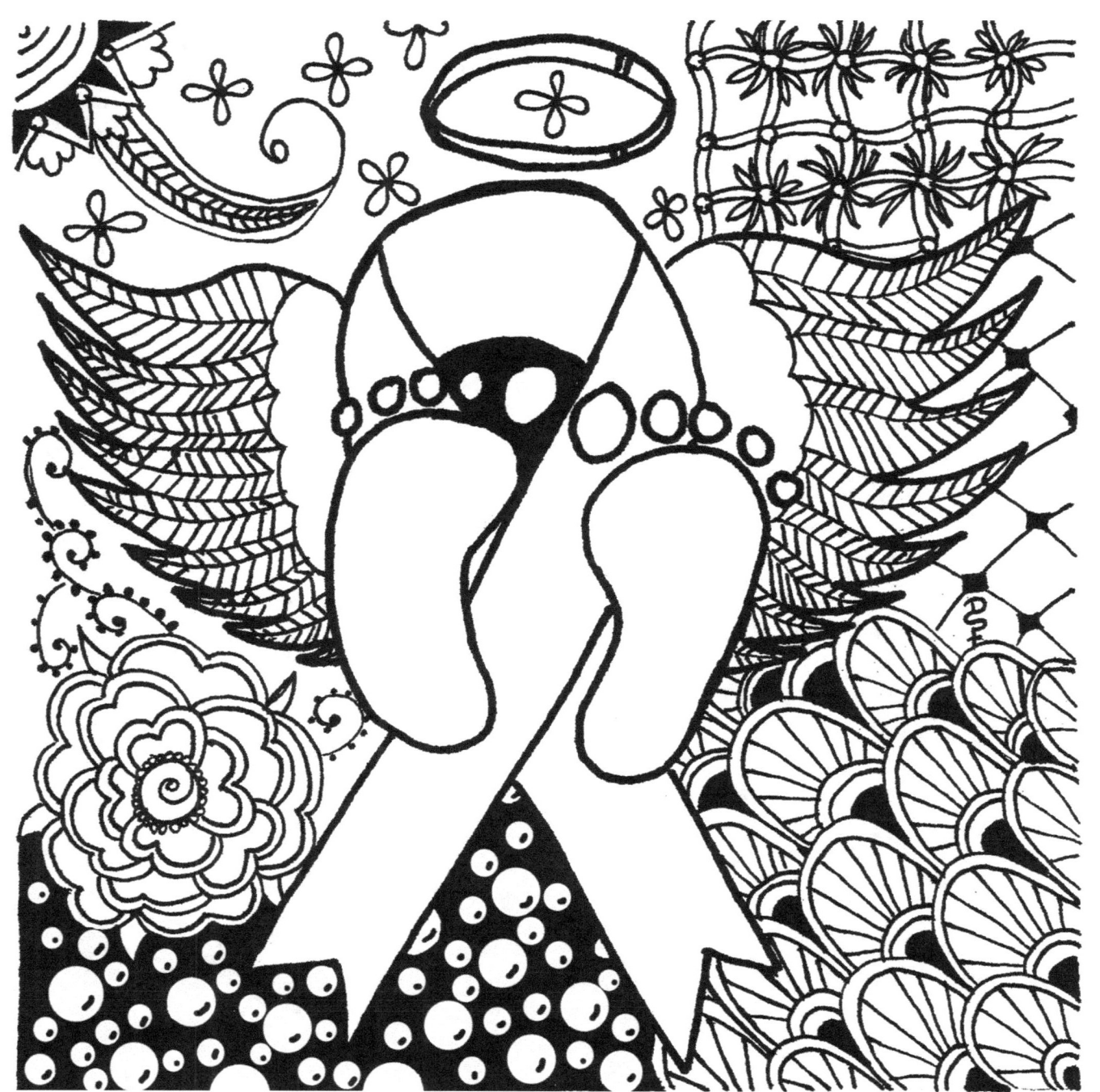

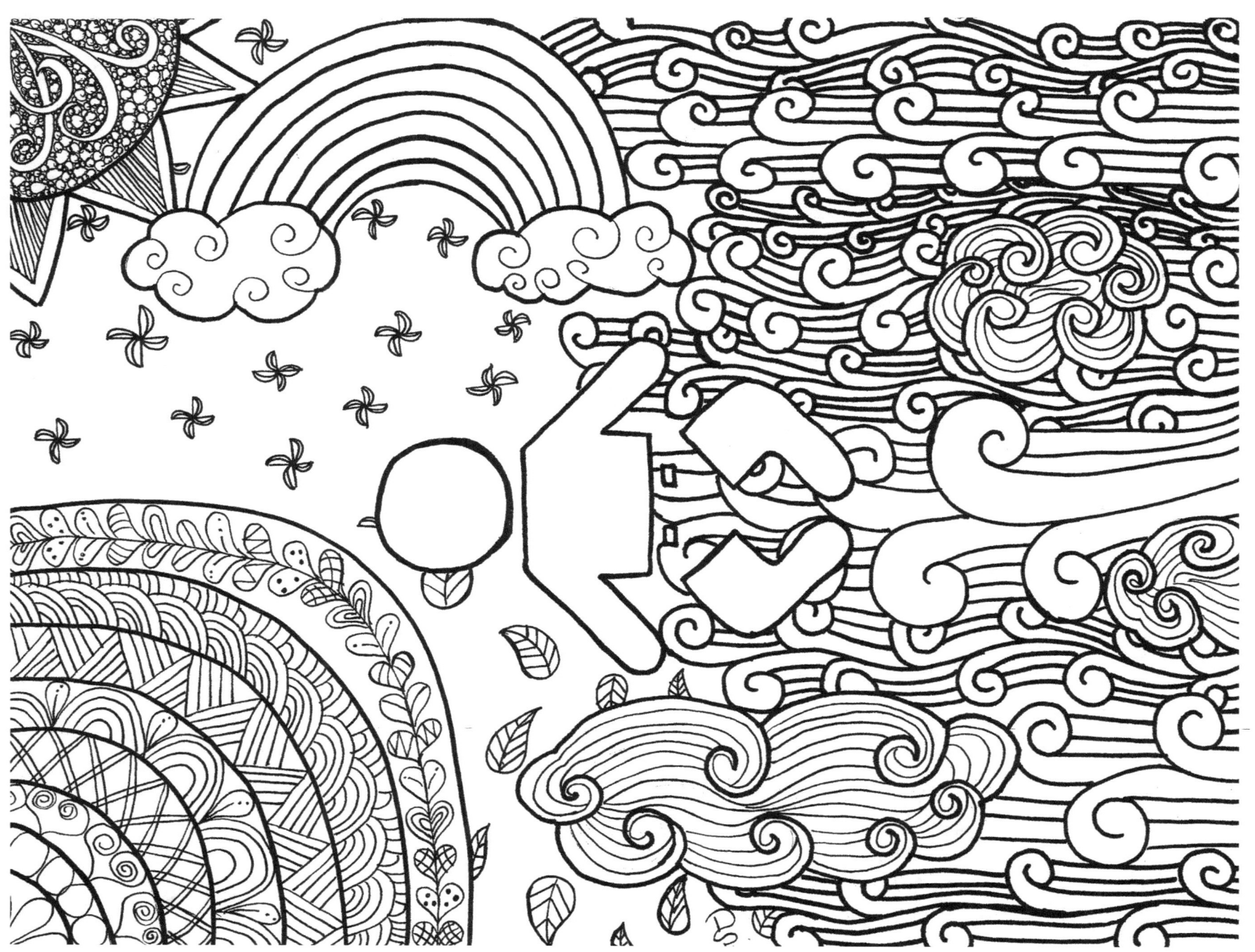

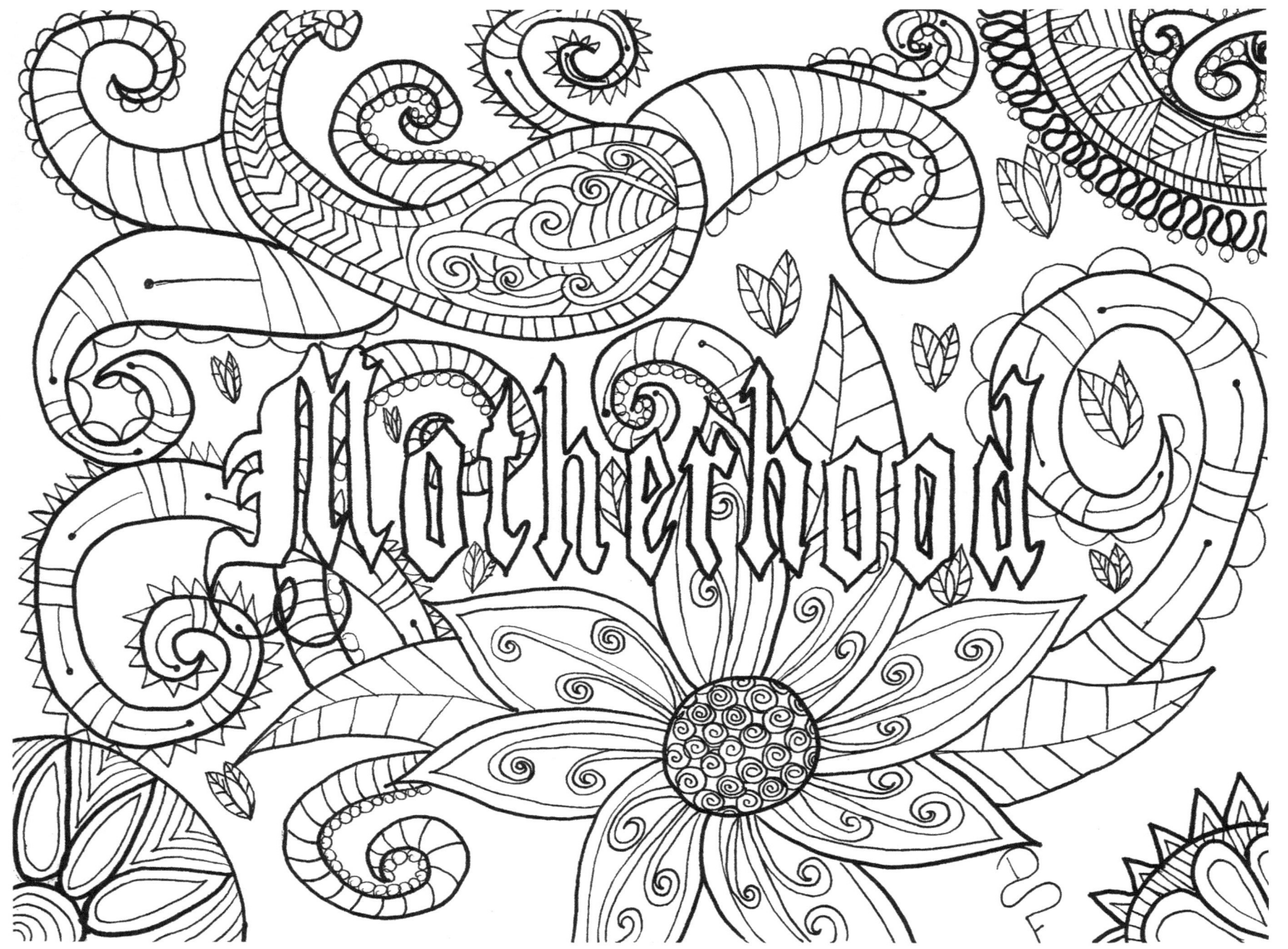

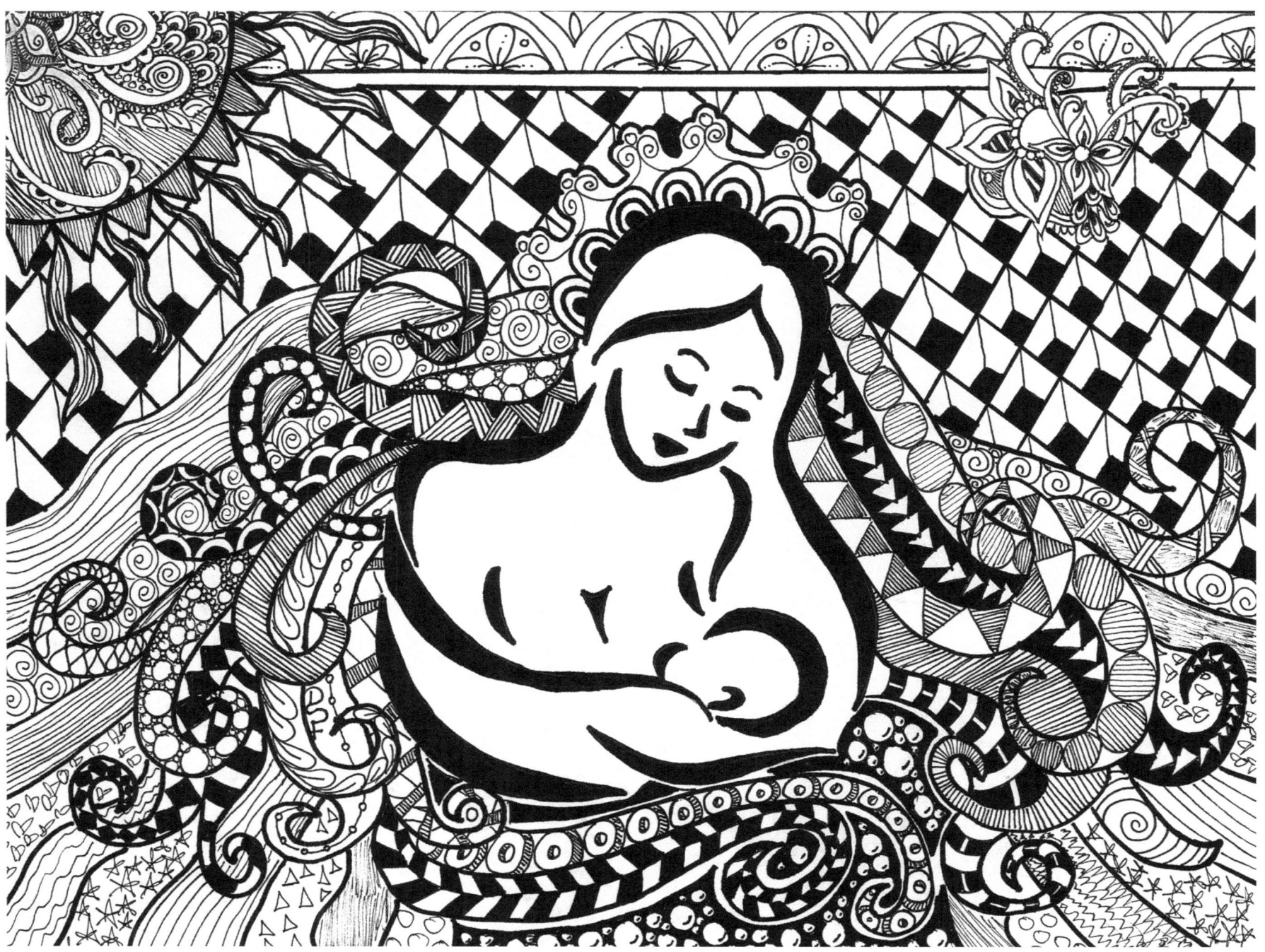

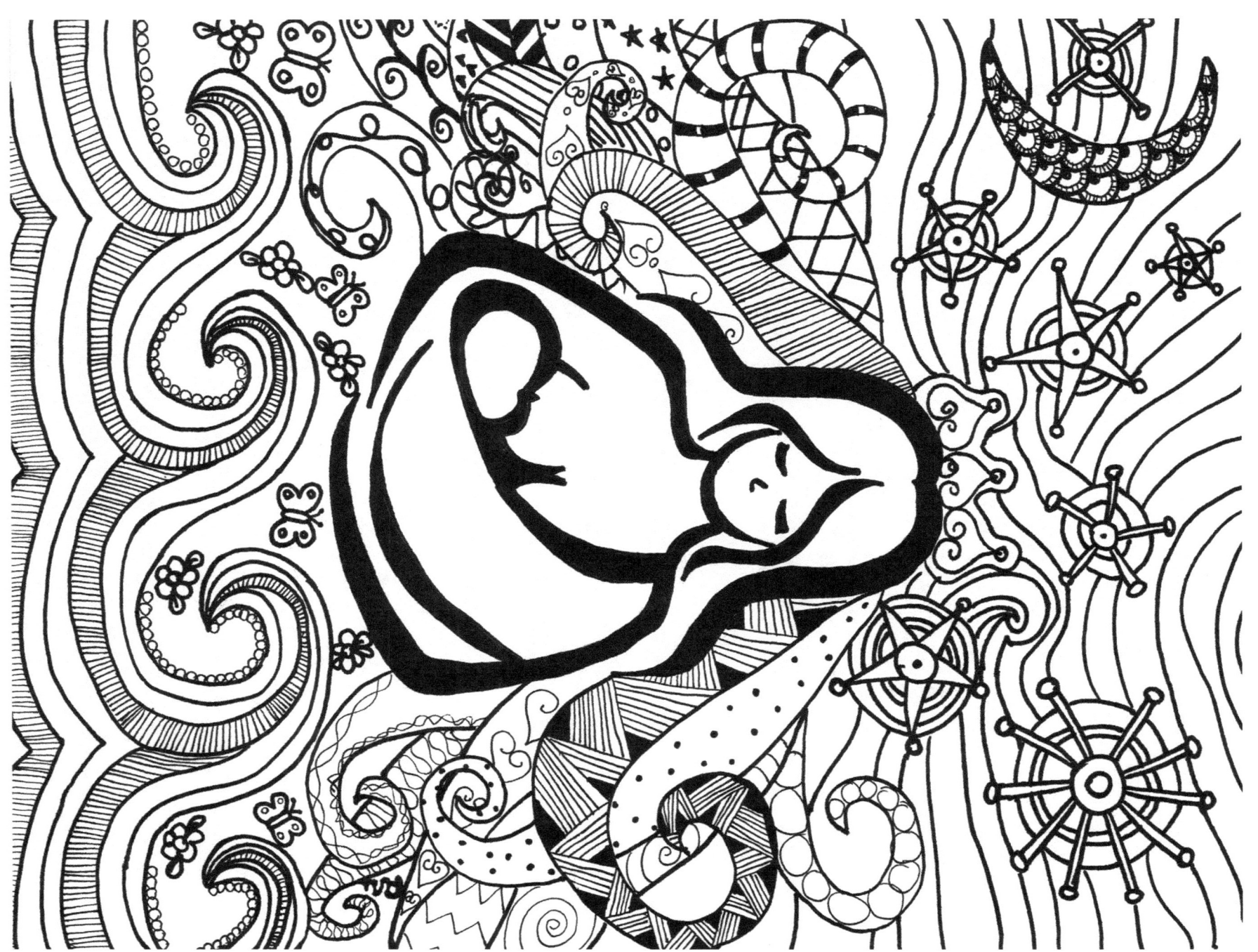

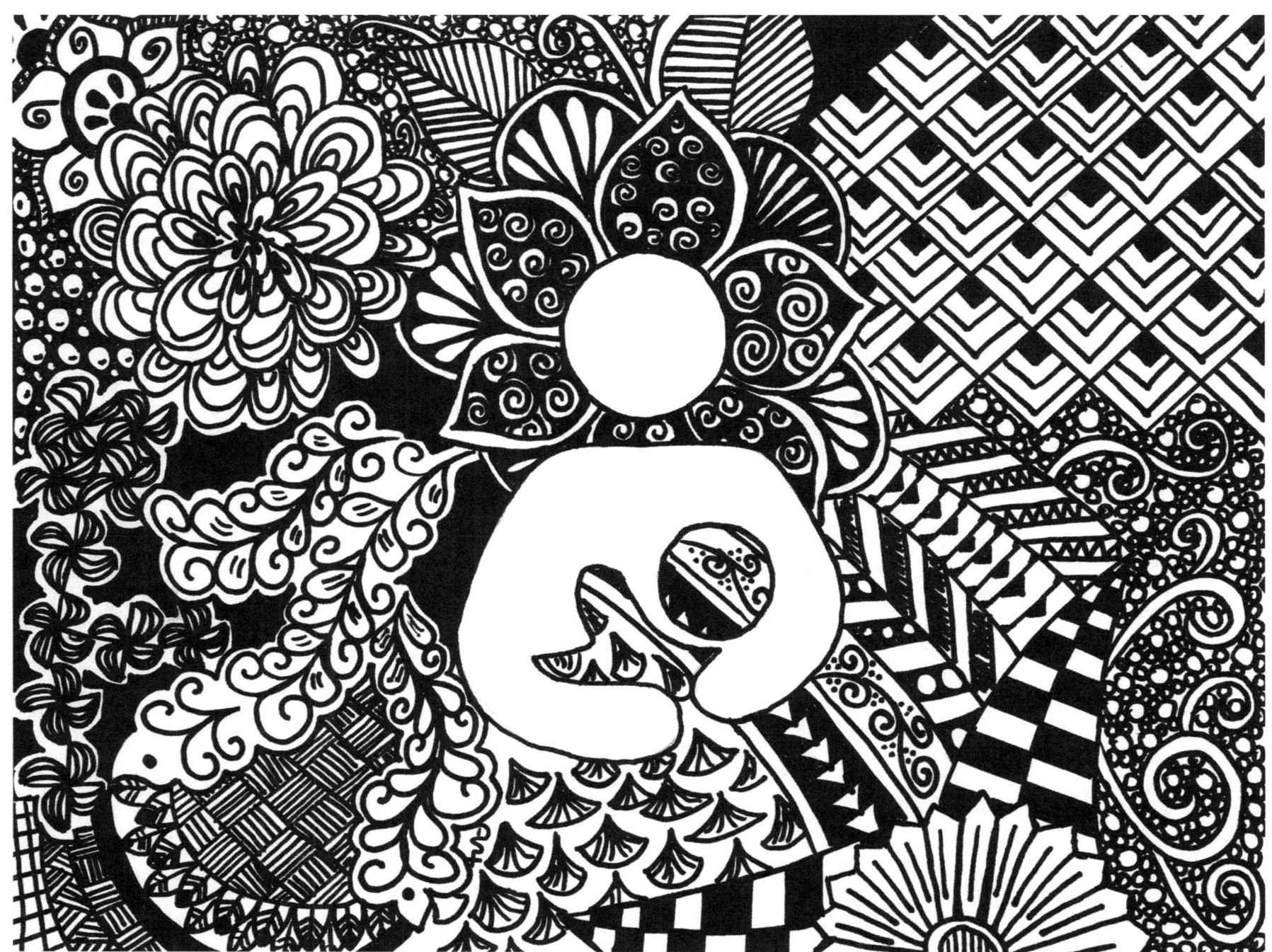

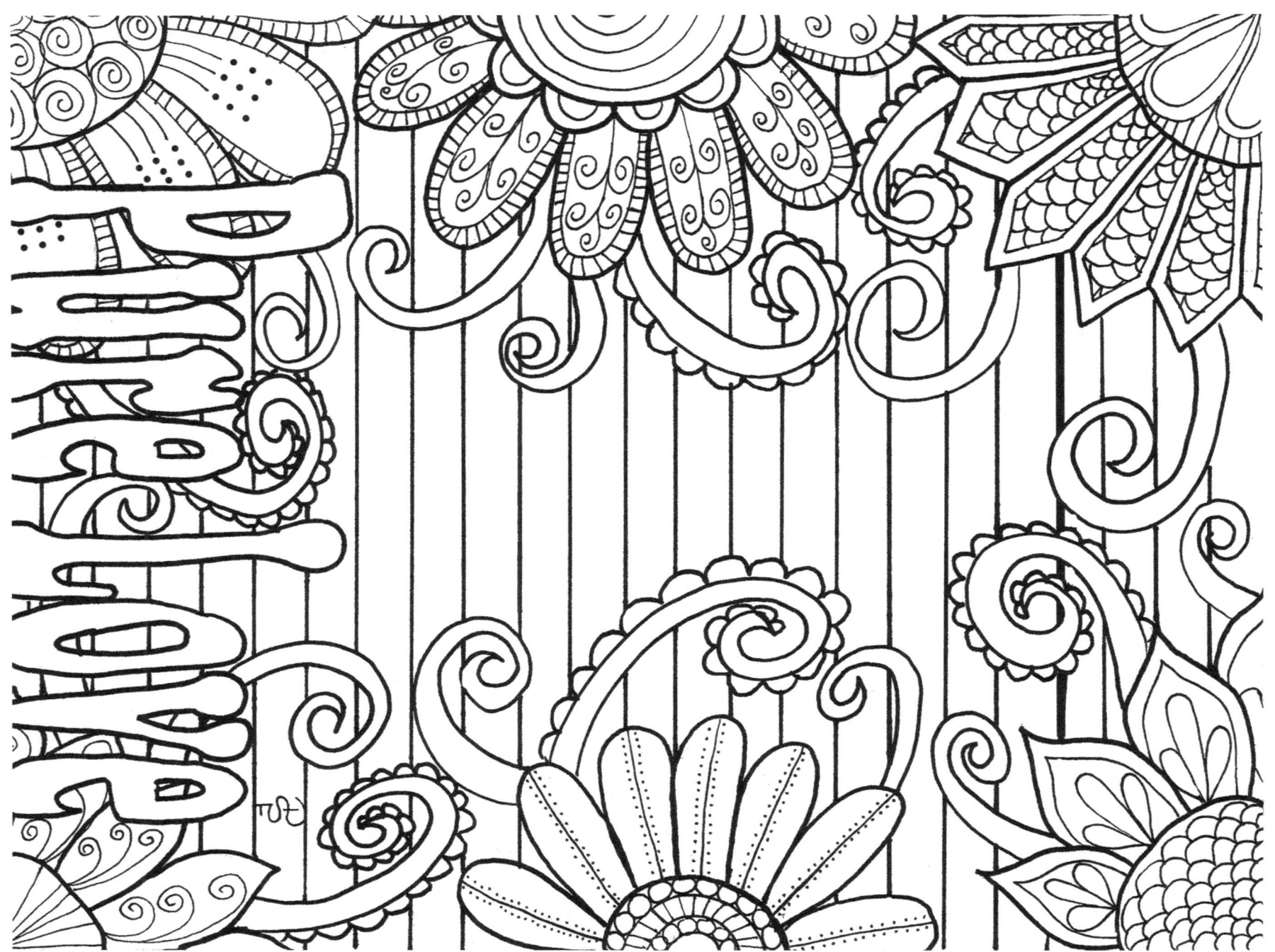

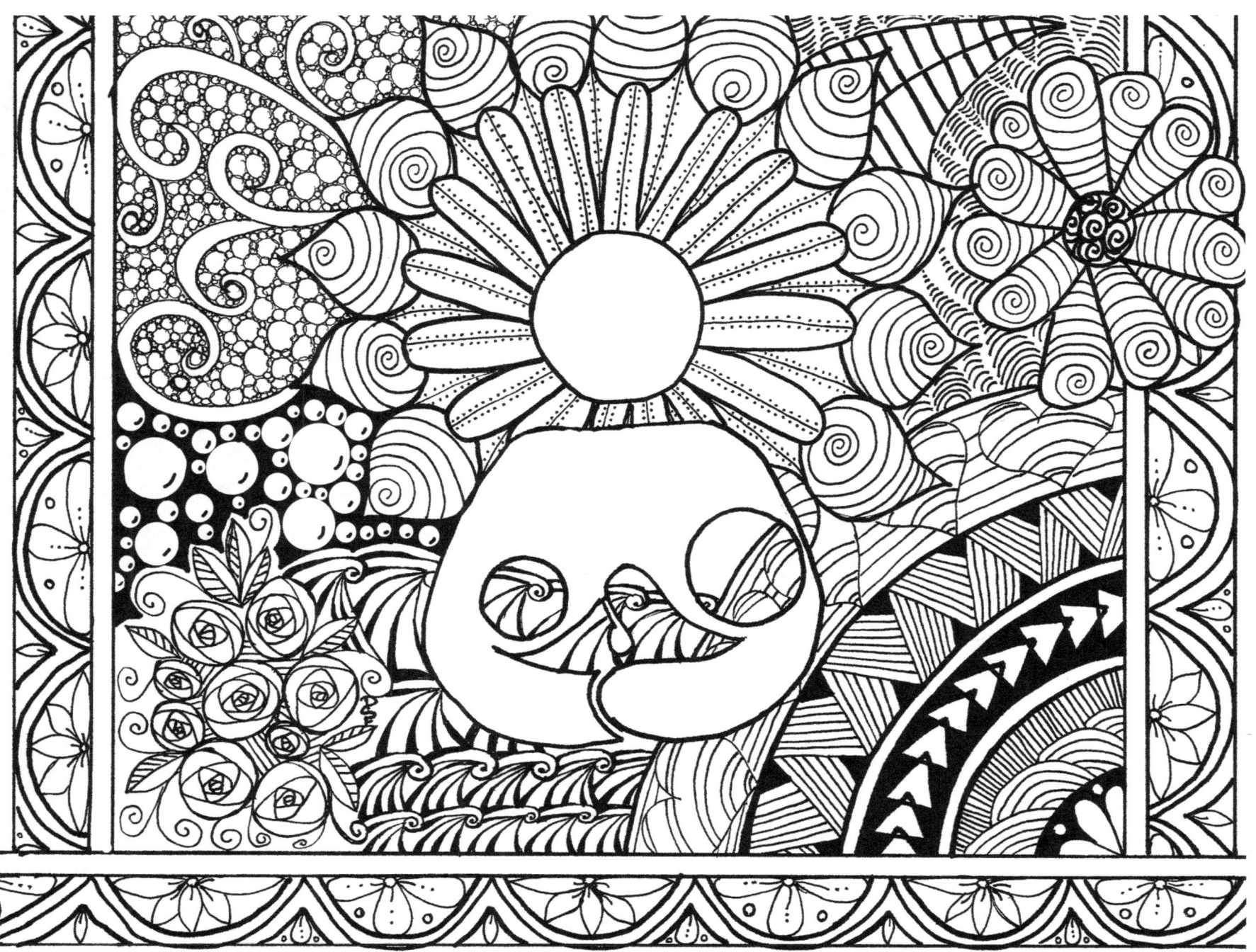

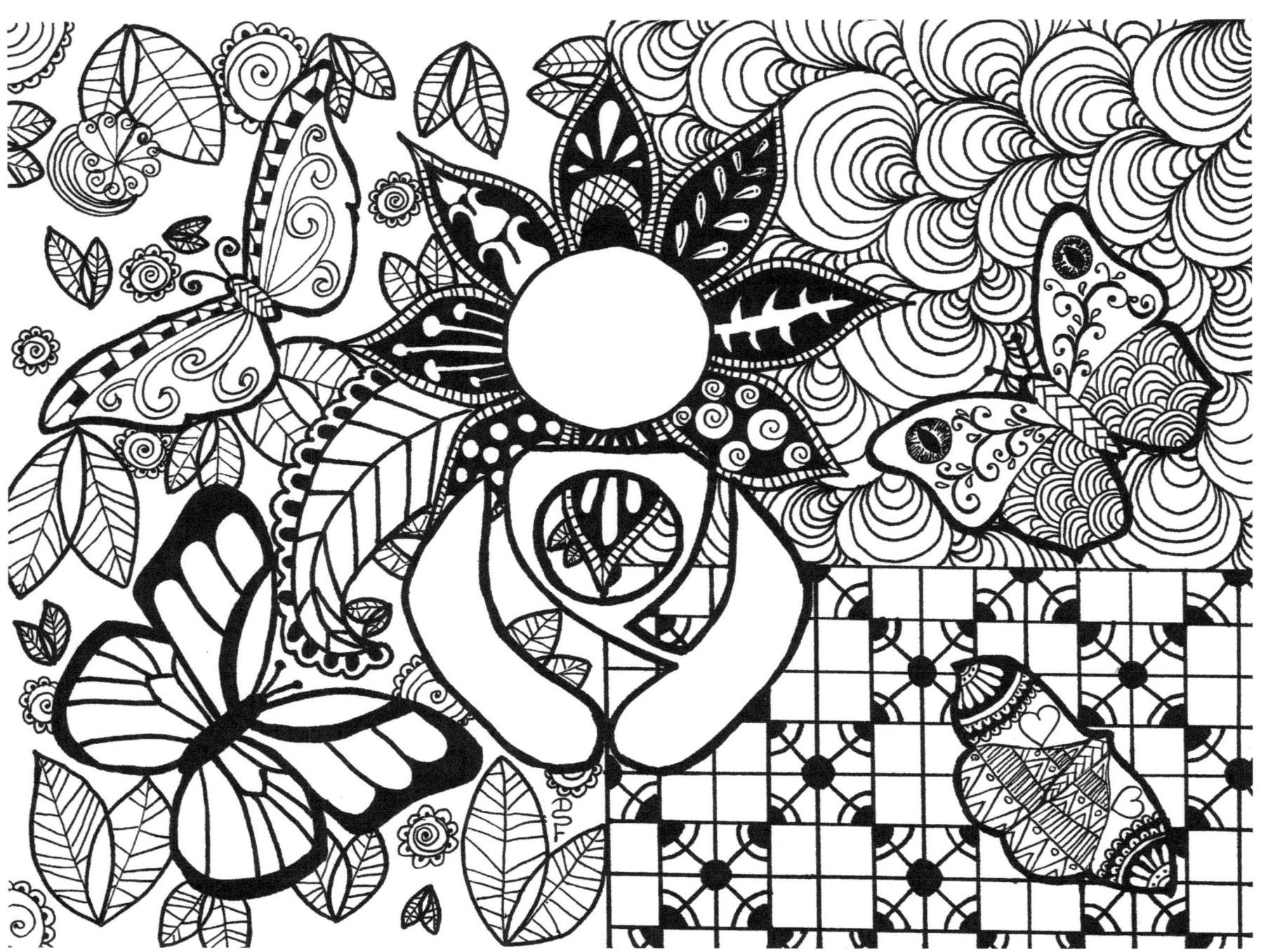

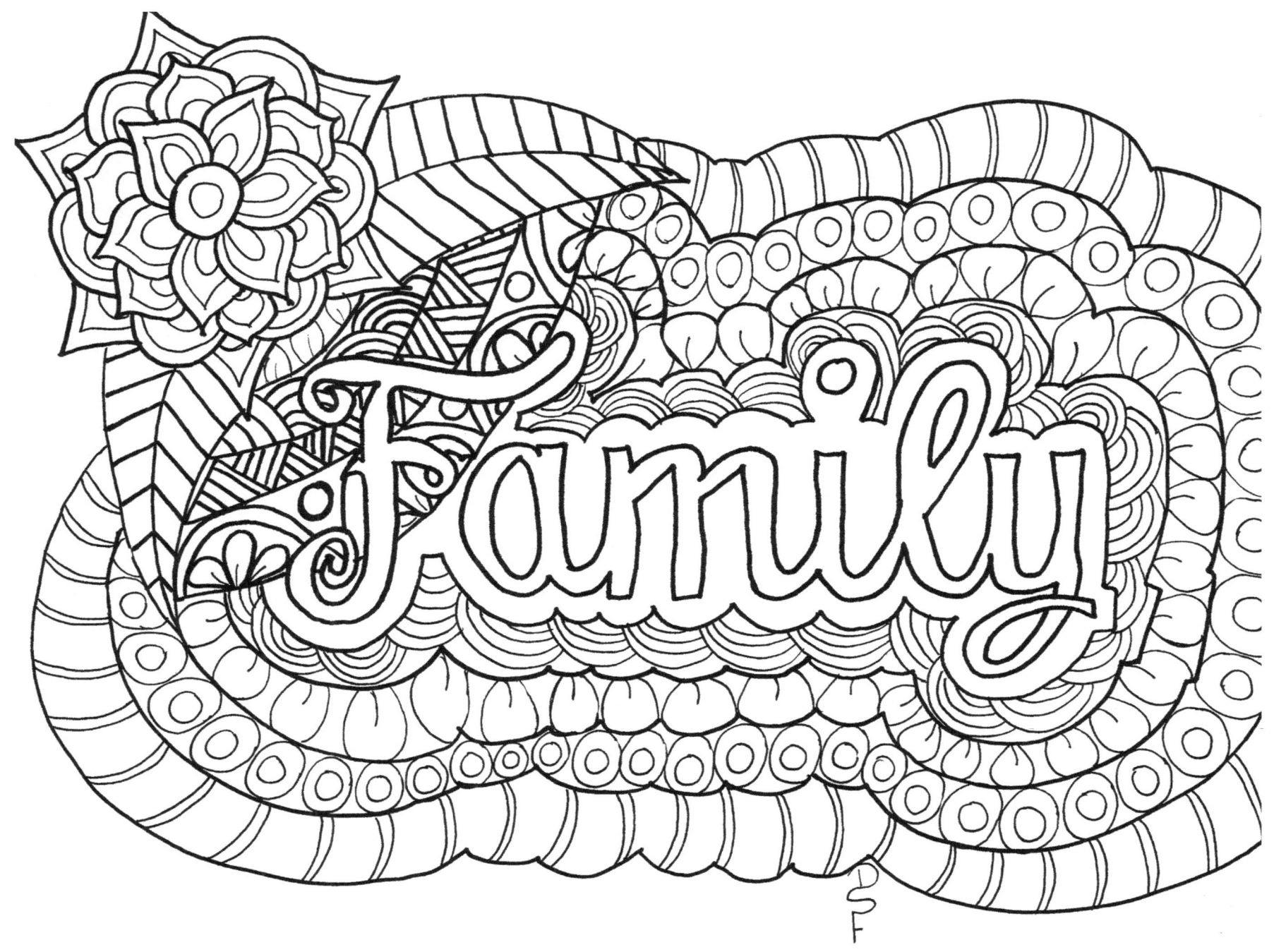

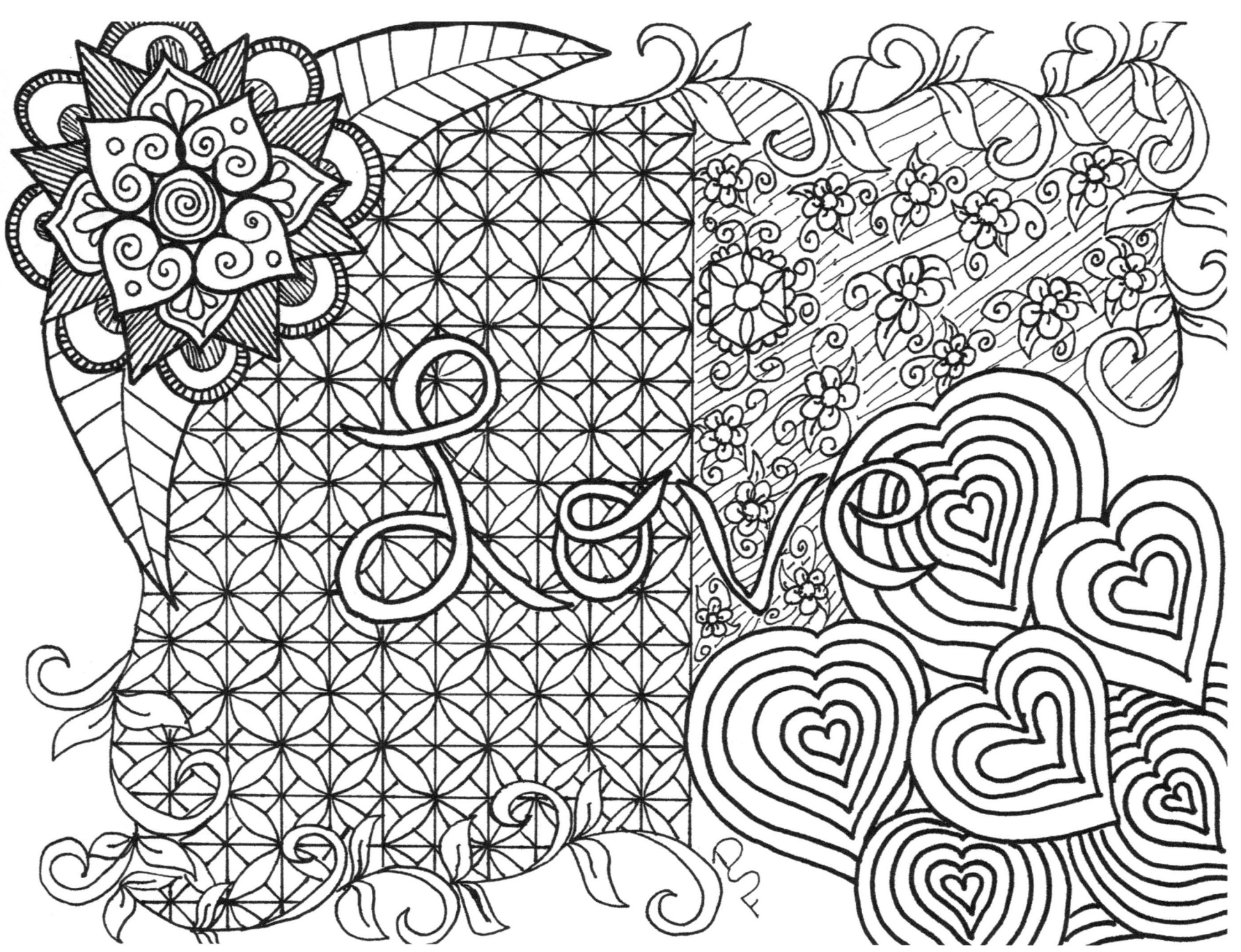

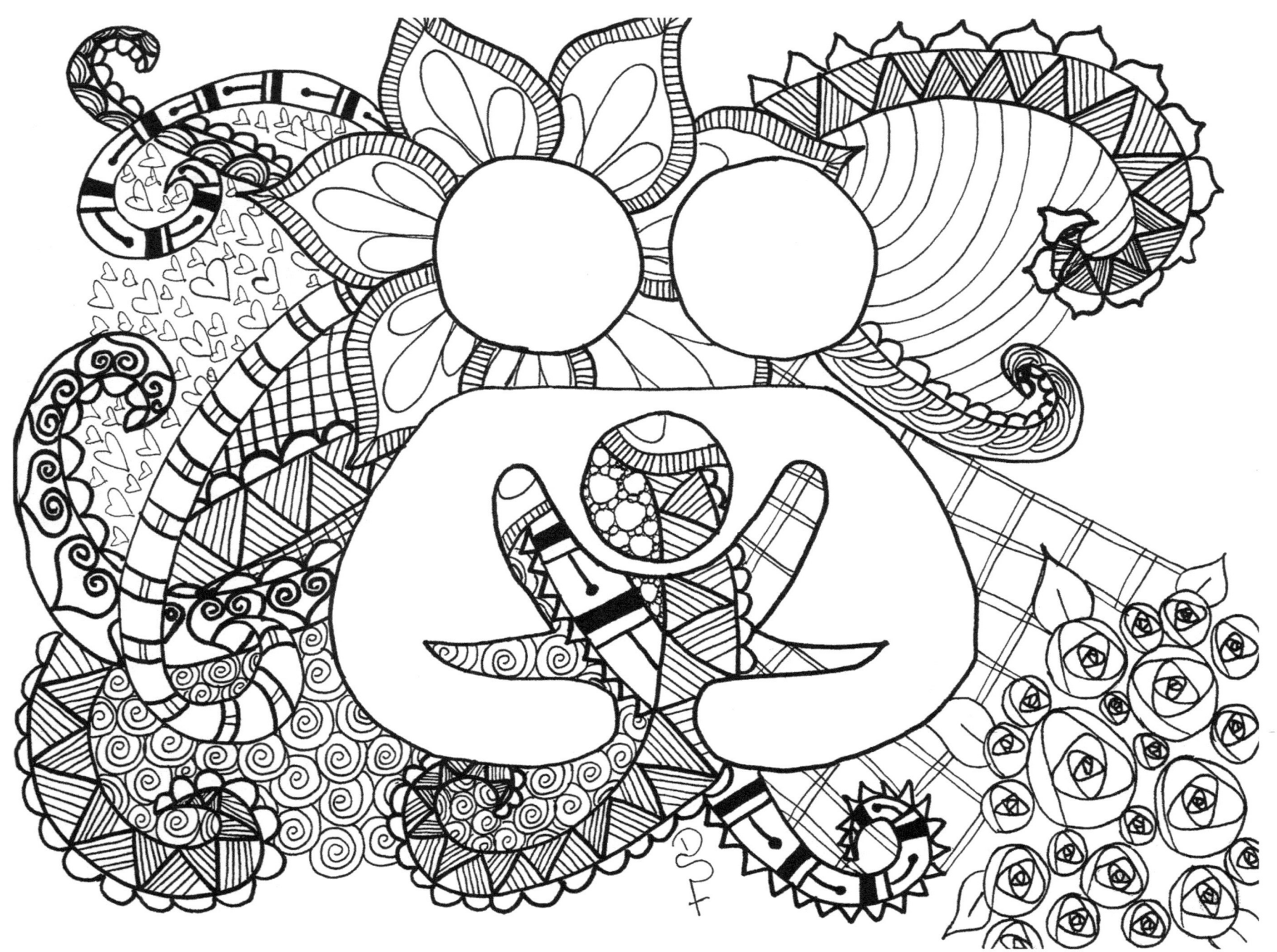

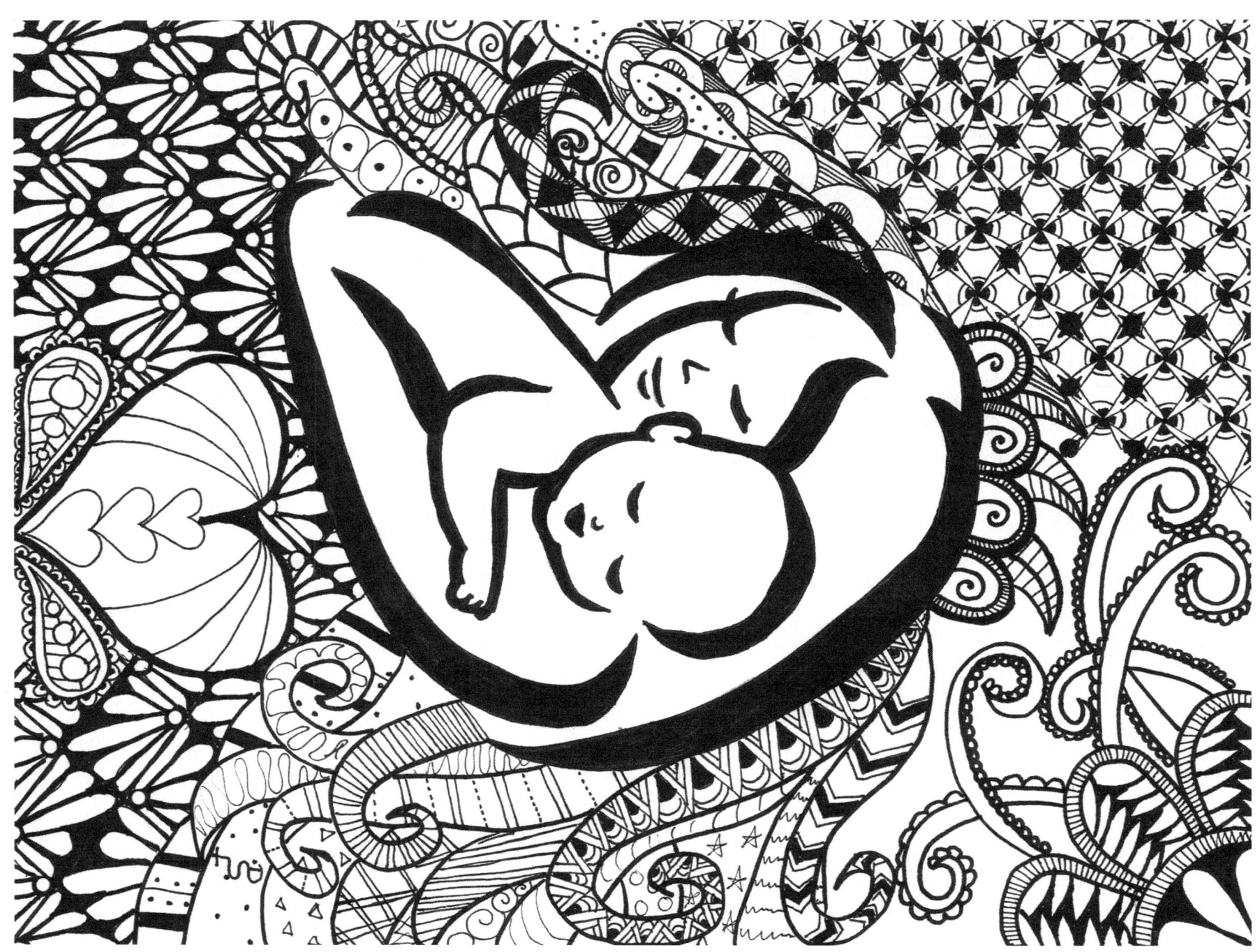

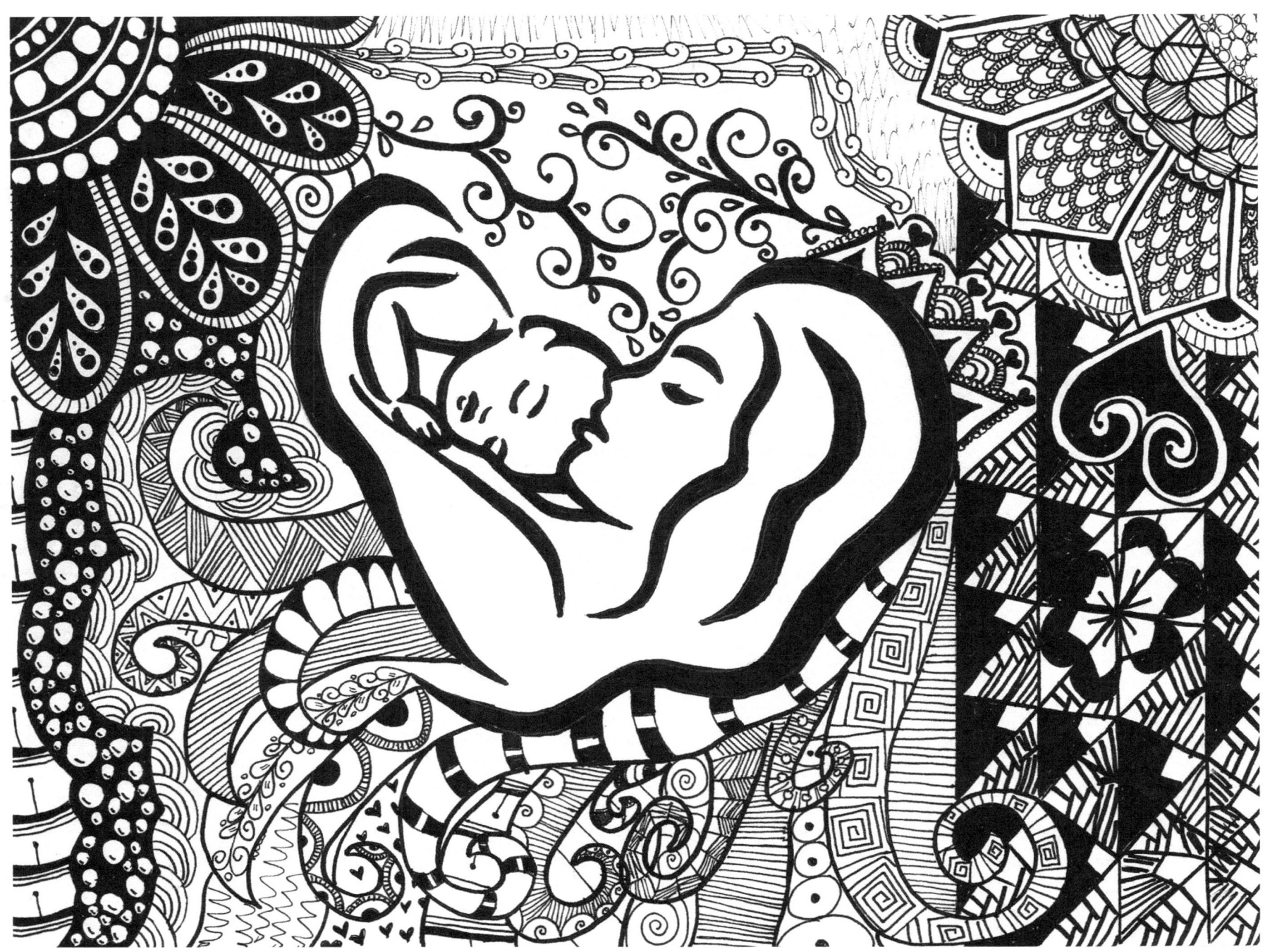

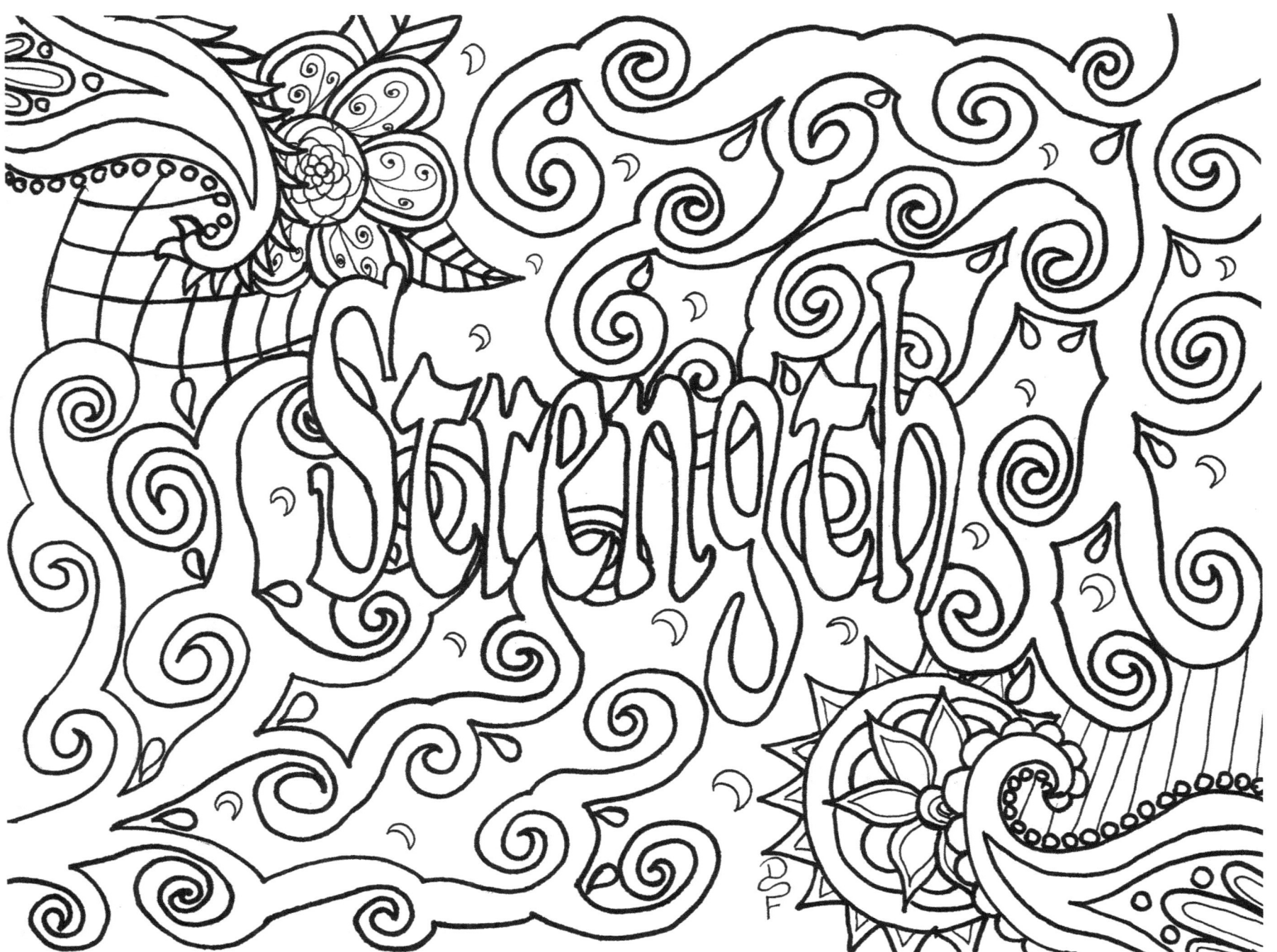

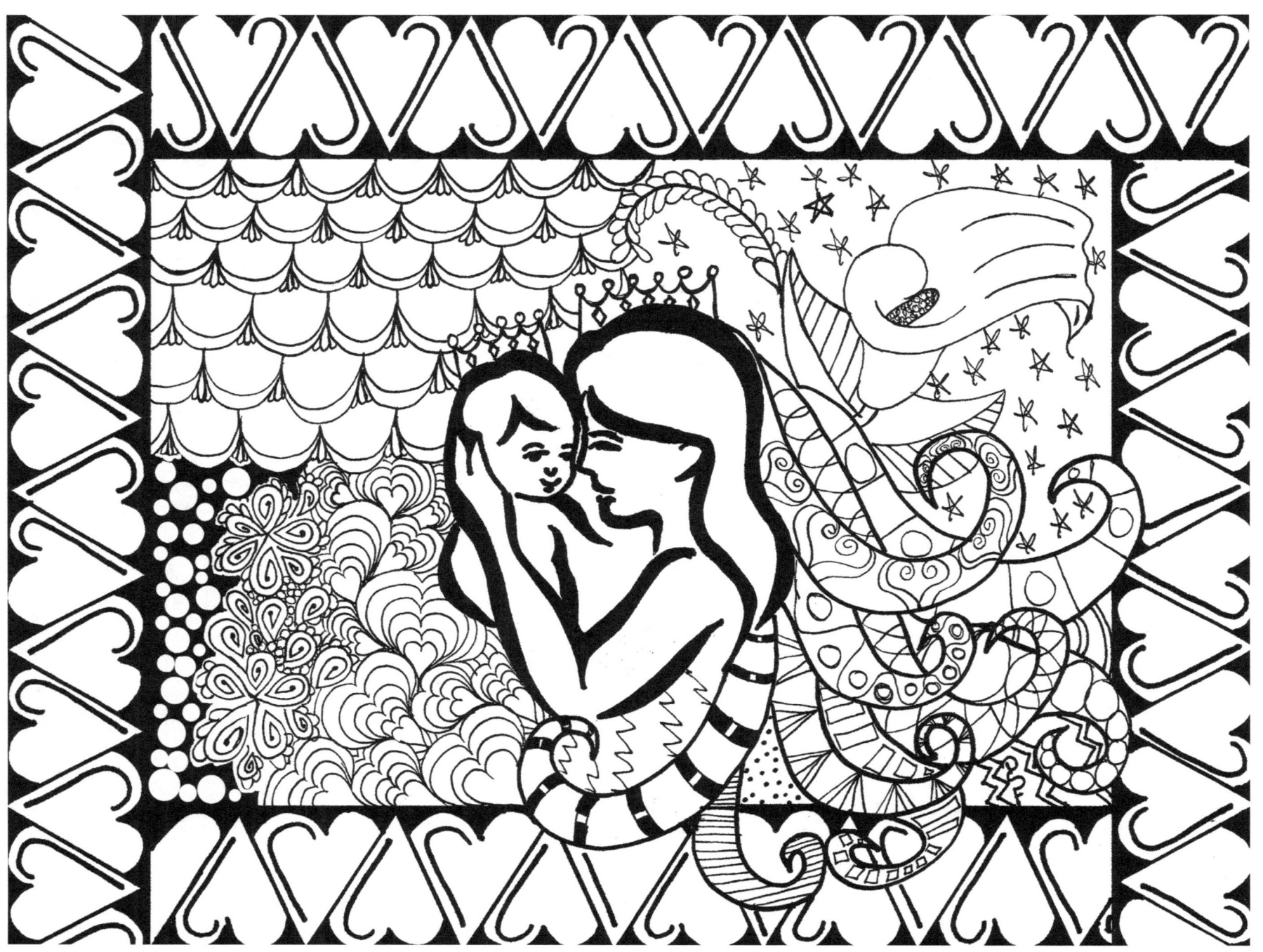

THANK YOU

I REALLY HOPE YOU ENJOYED THIS COLOR BOOK.
THANK YOU SO VERY MUCH FOR BUYING IT, AND
ENJOYING IT. IF YOU ENJOYED THIS BOOK LET ME KNOW.
I HOPE TO DO MORE WITH THE SAME THEME IN THE FUTURE.
PLEASE SHARE YOUR BEAUTIFUL COLORINGS OF MY
BOOK ON MY FACEBOOK PAGE.
THANK YOU AGAIN.